EDGE
BOOKS

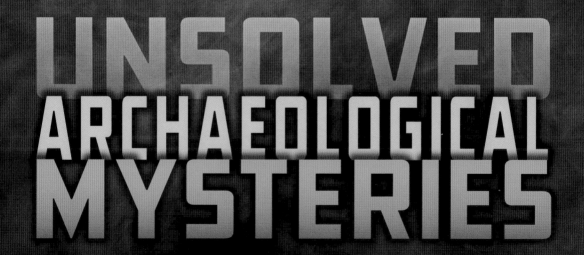

UNSOLVED
ARCHAEOLOGICAL
MYSTERIES

1710 Roe Crest Drive, North Mankato, Minnesota 56003
www.capstonepub.com

Library of Congress Cataloging-in-Publication Data
Capek, Michael.
Unsolved archaeological mysteries / by Michael Capek.
pages cm.—(Edge books. Unsolved mystery files)
Summary: "Describes mysterious and unsolved archaeological sites and artifacts from around the
world"—Provided by publisher.
Includes bibliographical references and index.
ISBN 978-1-4914-4262-3 (library binding)
ISBN 978-1-4914-4338-5 (paperback)
ISBN 978-1-4914-4318-7 (ebook PDF)
1. Archaeology—Juvenile literature. 2. Antiquities—Juvenile literature.
3. Excavations (Archaeology)—Juvenile literature. 4. Archaeologists—Juvenile literature. I. Title.
CC171.C37 2016
930.1—dc23   2015001431

Editorial Credits
Aaron Sautter, editor; Sarah Bennett, designer; Gina Kammer,
media researcher; Morgan Walters, production specialist

Photo Credits
Alamy: © Martin Bennett, 22-23; Corbis: © Charles O'Rear, 15; Dreamstime: © Galina Barskaya,
8-9; Glow Images: Superstock, 29; iStockphoto: wieditmedia, 27; Science Source: RIA Novosti, 17;
Shutterstock: Adwo, cover, Amy Nichole Harris, 6, Anton_Ivanov, (background) 4-5, ChameleonsEye,
5, David Bukach, 24-25, dmitry_islentev, 10-11, Pablo Hidalgo - Fotos593, 13, Pecold, 28, Stas Moroz
(background), 14-15, 16-17, William Silver, 18-19, 21

Design elements:
Shutterstock: Background Land, (faded background), Claire McAdams, (fog smoky background),
imageZebra, (Nazca line art), Mark Heider, (Earth map), MisterElements, (ink splatters), Peter
Hermes Furian, (Celtic spirals)

Contents

History Detectives

Archaeologists crouch, sweating in the blazing sun. They carefully move dirt and sand with **trowels** and small brushes. They're hot and tired, but they keep digging. Farmers here recently found pieces of pottery with bright red markings on them. As they dig deeper, the scientists find more pottery and some stone tools. Someone lived in this place long ago. But who? Perhaps they left behind more clues to explain who they were and how they lived.

Archaeologists are like history detectives. They search for clues and use the newest technology to examine every scrap of evidence. They piece it all together and keep digging for more. They want to learn how ancient people lived. But sometimes archaeologists are unable to find any answers. Some ancient artifacts and sites can't be explained.

archaeologist—a scientist who studies how people lived in the past

trowel—a hand tool with a flat blade

Who created the giant stone statues on a remote Pacific island, and why? Who was the mysterious Ice Maiden? Why did people in Peru draw giant pictures that can only be clearly seen from the sky? Keep reading to learn more about these and other archaeological mysteries that have baffled scientists for years.

Archaeologists carefully dig for artifacts at an ancient site in Qumran, Israel.

The Case of the Moving Moai

If you travel to Easter Island in the Pacific Ocean, you'll discover a strange sight. Scattered around the island are nearly 900 huge statues called moai (MO-eye). The giant stone figures stand an average of 14 feet (4.3 meters) tall. The largest is nearly 69 feet (21 m) tall and weighs 270 tons (245 metric tons).

The odd statues have oversized heads with long, alienlike faces. They have large noses, puckered lips, droopy ears, and empty eye sockets. At one time, some of the statues also had huge red stone hats weighing many tons.

Settlers first arrived on the island between AD 1000 and 1200. People on Easter Island made the moai statues for about 600 years. But then they suddenly stopped. Nearly all of the secrets of the island and its statues died out with the people hundreds of years ago. History detectives have solved some mysteries surrounding Easter Island's statues. For example, archaeologists know where the statues were carved. They also believe the statues represent ancient kings, chiefs, or dead **ancestors**. However, many mysteries remain.

ancestor—a member of a person's family who lived a long time ago

7

Walking Statues?

Perhaps the biggest mystery involves how the statues were moved. Researchers have learned that many of the moai are miles away from where they were carved. Some experts think early people moved the statues on huge wooden sleds. The statues were first laid on the sleds, which were then rolled over round logs on the ground. Many people working together could have moved a large statue this way.

However, some Easter Island people remembered an old saying: "The moai walked." What does this mean? Some archaeologists think the early islanders had a way to "walk" the statues across the island. They would first tie ropes around a standing moai. Then a small army of workers could carefully rock it back and forth and side to side. This rocking motion would slowly tug a moai forward until it reached its final location. Archaeologists continue to study how the huge statues were moved. But for now, Easter Island's stony guardians aren't revealing their secrets.

Mystery of the Nazca Lines

In the 1920s and 1930s, airplane pilots discovered something incredible. While flying high over the Nazca Desert in southern Peru they saw huge shapes drawn in the sand. These included straight lines, triangles, circles, spirals, and **trapezoids**.

Visitors can see a few Nazca images by climbing a nearby observation tower.

These shapes can still be seen today. But even more amazing are the 70 gigantic drawings of various animals. Clearly visible are a spider, a hummingbird, a monkey, and many others. One drawing of a pelican is 900 feet (274 m) long! It's hard to believe these huge pictures hadn't been noticed before the 1920s. But then again, they're so large that they can only be seen clearly from hundreds of feet in the air.

Archaeologists have learned who made the pictures. The ancient Nazca people were farmers and herders. They lived in the area between 300 and 800 BC. Scientists also know the lines were made by moving dark colored stones to reveal the lighter ground underneath. From high above the pictures look similar to chalk drawings on a sidewalk.

trapezoid—a four-sided shape that has only one set of parallel sides

11

What Are They?

But the real question remains—why did the Nazca people create the giant pictures in the first place? After all, nobody on the ground can see the pictures clearly. Why would people make something no one on Earth could appreciate?

One explanation is that people may have created and used the lines as part of religious **rituals**. The huge drawings might have been gifts offered to the native people's gods. Walking along the lines while singing or chanting may have been a way for people to connect with the spirits. It's also possible that art was just an important part of Nazca **culture**. Pieces of Nazca pottery found nearby are decorated with similar shapes and drawings.

Some people have a more unusual theory to explain the lines. They think that aliens may have visited Earth in ancient times. These people think aliens may have used the straight lines as landing strips for their spaceships. They also think the giant pictures helped aliens know where to land. This theory may explain why some drawings are so large that they can even be seen from space!

High-Flying Ancients?

In the 1970s adventurer Jim Woodman proposed a new theory about the Nazca lines. He thought the ancient Nazca people might have flown high in balloons to help make their creations. To test this theory, he built a balloon made of dried grass and other materials available to the Nazca people. He then filled it with hot air from a fire pit similar to those found near the lines. Amazingly, his experiment worked! Woodman soared to 300 feet (91 m) high and landed safely. But many experts say he was just lucky. Strong winds in the area make such flights risky and dangerous. There's no solid evidence that the ancient people made hot air balloons.

ritual—a ceremony involving a set of religious actions

culture—a people's way of life, ideas, customs, and traditions

Siberia's Frozen Ice Maiden

It's 1993 and Russian archaeologists are opening a **tomb** in Siberia's Altai Mountains. They know of old stories that describe tough Scythian warriors who once lived in this area. However, some historians have said the Scythian people were likely just a legend created by early writers. The archaeologists think that opening the tomb might finally solve the mystery.

When they open the tomb, they find that it's frozen into a solid block of ice. They pour boiling water over the ice to melt it. Once inside, they find a coffin decorated with shapes of deer and snow leopards. Inside the coffin is the body of a young woman. Tests later show that the mysterious woman was buried nearly 2,500 years ago. She was about 25 years old when she died. The archaeologists call the young woman the "Ice Maiden."

The woman was clearly a special person to the people who buried her. She was wearing a fancy **headdress** decorated with gold and wooden birds. She was also wearing a colorful dress made of wool and camel's hair and a silk shirt. Tattoos on her arms showed pictures of flowers and mythological animals. Everything shows that the woman was rich and much loved. But was she a Scythian?

The Ice Maiden was found in a small wooden tomb inside a burial mound known as a kurgan.

tomb—a grave, room, or building that holds a dead body

headdress—a decorative covering for the head

Examining the Evidence

The archaeologists also found the remains of six horses and their saddles buried with the Ice Maiden. The old stories said that Scythian women fought alongside men as warriors. Perhaps the Ice Maiden was a warrior. However, there were also many items only a rich or important person would have owned. For example, there was a bright red pouch with a mirror inside, as well as a drinking cup made from a yak's horn. The Maiden's fine clothes and the rich objects in her tomb didn't reflect a warrior's life. Perhaps she was a princess or an important priestess.

The woman's tattoos may be another important clue. Some experts think the tattoos may have had important religious meaning to her. Perhaps her people thought the images could help them identify one another after death. Others think the Ice Maiden could have been an important storyteller. She may have worn the pictures to help illustrate the tales she told.

The Ice Maiden's tattoos are some of the most detailed designs ever found on an ancient body.

Whoever she was, the woman's burial was important to her people. They carried her and many of her belongings high into the mountains to be buried. It's said that the Scythians performed this burial practice for their important leaders. Archaeologists feel the evidence points to the woman being one of the ancient Scythian people. However, there's no way to be completely certain. The mystery of the Ice Maiden's identity may never be fully solved.

The Riddle of Chaco Canyon

Chaco Canyon in northwestern New Mexico doesn't seem like a nice place to live. The rocky landscape is harsh and dry. It's blazing hot in the summer, and winters are bone-chillingly cold.

However, about 1,000 years ago Chaco Canyon was home to a thriving culture. The Chaco people lived in this 10-mile- (16-km-) long canyon from about AD 850 to 1250. During that time they built hundreds of stone buildings in several small villages.

At least nine large buildings, called Great Houses, can be found in Chaco Canyon. The largest of these stood five stories high and had hundreds of rooms. It could have housed several thousand people. Along with the Great Houses, the Chaco people built dozens of structures known as **kivas**. These large underground rooms were often two stories deep and up to 45 feet (13.7 m) wide.

The Chaco people also built an amazing system of roads to connect the nearby villages together. These roads stretched up to 400 miles (644 km) from the canyon in all directions. The roads brought a steady stream of people, building materials, food, and other items into the canyon.

kiva—an underground room once used by American Indians for special ceremonies

A Lost Civilization

Evidence shows that Chaco Canyon was likely a busy trading center that drew people from all over the region. However, people stopped coming to Chaco Canyon in the late 1100s. They began living, trading, and practicing their religion elsewhere. By the mid-1200s almost all the people had left.

Why did the people abandon Chaco Canyon? Some experts think people left because of changes in their religious beliefs or to escape enemy attacks. But many scientists believe there is a better answer to the mystery. By studying nearby tree rings, they found that a series of severe **droughts** hit the area in the 1200s. With little rainfall it became difficult to grow enough food to feed everyone. The people likely left to join other communities. Nobody knows the full reasons why the Chaco people left. But the buildings and other structures they left behind are reminders of a once great civilization.

Where Did the Chaco People Go?

Historians believe the Chacoans split into several smaller groups of people. These became the Anasazi, Pueblo, Zuni, Hopi, Navaho, and other American Indian tribes. These tribes have lived in the area for hundreds of years. Many Indians still see Chaco Canyon as a sacred place. They believe the spirits of their ancestors still roam there.

STAY ON TRAIL
KEEP OFF WALLS

drought—a long period of weather with little or no rainfall

The Avebury Puzzle

The circle of stones at Avebury, in Wiltshire, England, is a huge and fascinating puzzle. It's the largest stone **henge** in the world. It's 1,401 feet (427 m) in diameter, which makes it 16 times bigger than England's famous Stonehenge.

A huge dirt embankment once surrounded the site. This circular dirt structure stood more than 20 feet (6 m) tall and was 1,410 feet (430 m) wide. Inside the dirt wall was a 30-foot- (9-m-) deep ditch. About 100 huge stones stood around the inner edge of the ditch. Two smaller stone circles sat inside these massive earthworks. Each of the smaller circles was nearly as large as Stonehenge and had about 30 standing stones.

henge—a circular area enclosed by a dirt bank or ditch and surrounded by large stones or wooden posts

The Avebury site was built during the late Stone Age around 2500 BC. Archaeologists have found hundreds of ancient picks and shovels while exploring the area. These tools were made from deer antlers and oxen shoulder blades. Digging such a huge ditch with these crude tools was likely very hard. But moving the monument's huge stones would have been even harder. Many of the stones weighed more than 10 tons (9 metric tons) and had to be dragged from several miles away.

A Planned Landscape?

Why did the ancient people build this huge monument? Experts' best guess is that Avebury and sites like it were once used as gathering places. Archaeologists have found ancient roads, or avenues, that once connected Avebury to other nearby sites. These include the West Kennett Long **Barrow** and another stone circle named The Sanctuary. Silbury Hill, another mysterious site, is also located near Avebury.

While visiting each of these locations, people can see one or more of the other nearby sites. For this reason, experts think these places form a kind of "planned landscape." It's possible the area around Avebury formed a type of religious center for prehistoric people. It may have even stretched as far away as Stonehenge, which sits about 20 miles (32 kilometers) to the south.

barrow—a mound of earth made to cover a grave in prehistoric times

Where did the missing stones go?

Evidence shows that some of the stones from Avebury might have been moved to Stonehenge. Scientists aren't sure when or why ancient people did this. But in the 1100s, Christians thought the circle of stones was evil. They didn't like the idea that ancient people may have worshipped pagan gods among the stones. They tried to destroy the monument by knocking over many of the stones and smashing them to pieces.

Ireland's Strange Newgrange Tomb

Sitting on hills overlooking the Boyne River in Ireland are a group of cavelike tombs. People have whispered about these spooky tombs for hundreds of years. They were built about 5,000 years ago, making them older than the pyramids in Egypt. They are all eerie, but the Newgrange tomb may be the most mysterious.

One of Newgrange's most puzzling features is the small, rectangular opening above the entrance. Known as the "roof-box," this opening looks similar to a skylight over many modern doors.

What would be the purpose of building a window in an ancient tomb? Archaeologists studied the opening and found that it had an amazing alignment. Each year on the **winter solstice**, the first rays of the rising sun shine directly through this small opening. A narrow beam of light shoots straight down the tomb's passageway. The whole chamber remains brilliantly lit for 17 minutes.

winter solstice—the day of the year when the sun rises at its northernmost point

How did the ancient people build Newgrange in such perfect alignment with the rising sun? To build it today, people would likely use computers and modern equipment to line it up with the sun. But ancient people built it using only stone, wood, and bone tools.

Spirals in the Stone

Many of the stones at Newgrange are decorated with prehistoric artwork. Double spiral shapes are the most common. One massive stone at the tomb's entrance is covered with them. This spiral shape is also carved into the back wall of the tomb. The first light of the sun on the solstice falls directly on these markings. This shape clearly had special importance to the ancient builders.

What were the spirals for? Why was the tomb built to let in sunlight on the solstice? Did people wait inside to watch the sunrise? Or did the ancient builders believe that sunlight on the solstice was somehow important to the dead?

Some scientists think ancient people used Newgrange's roof-box to track the beginning of the new year.

Nobody knows the answers to the questions surrounding Newgrange and other mysterious sites around the world. It's possible that the answers may never be known. But historians and archaeologists will keep asking questions and digging for the truth.

Glossary

ancestor (AN-sess-tur)—a member of a person's family who lived a long time ago

archaeologist (ar-kee-OL-uh-jist)—a scientist who studies how people lived in the past

barrow (BA-roh)—a mound of earth made to cover a grave in prehistoric times

culture (KUHL-chuhr)—a people's way of life, ideas, customs, and traditions

drought (DROUT)—a long period of weather with little or no rainfall

headdress (HED-dres)—a decorative covering for the head

henge (HENJ)—a circular area enclosed by a dirt bank or ditch and surrounded by large stones or wooden posts

kiva (KEE-vuh)—an underground room once used by Native Americans for special ceremonies

mythological (mith-uh-LOJ-uh-kuhl)—having to do with mythology

ritual (RICH-oo-uhl)—a ceremony involving a set of religious actions

tomb (TOOM)—a grave, room, or building that holds a dead body

trapezoid (TRAP-uh-zoyd)—a four-sided shape that has only one set of parallel sides

trowel (TROU-uhl)—a hand tool with a flat blade

winter solstice (WIN-tur SOL-stiss)—the day of the year when the sun rises at its northernmost point

Read More

Barber, Nicola. *Lost Cities.* Treasure Hunters. Chicago: Capstone Raintree, 2013.

Bow, James. *Hidden Worlds.* Mystery Files. New York: Crabtree Publishing Company, 2013.

Fay, Gail. *Secrets of Mesa Verde: Cliff Dwellings of the Pueblo.* Archaeological Mysteries. North Mankato, Minn.: Capstone Press, 2015.

Internet Sites

FactHound offers a safe, fun way to find Internet sites related to this book. All of the sites on FactHound have been researched by our staff.

Here's all you do:

Visit *www.facthound.com*

Type in this code: 9781491442623

 Check out projects, games and lots more at **www.capstonekids.com**

Index